How to Play
SOLITAIRE

Publications International, Ltd.

SOLITAIRE GAMES

The challenging games presented in this book will sharpen your strategic skills during time spent alone. Attempt one or two of them when you take some time out during the day to refresh your mind or maybe as you wind down at night.

KLONDIKE

One of the oldest and most popular games of solitaire is Klondike, which is commonly thought of as simply "Solitaire." It is also the solitaire game usually played on the computer.

The object

To uncover the four aces, to create foundations for each suit by starting them with the aces, and to build the foundation of each suit to the king sequentially

The cards

Standard 52-card deck

4

Dealing to the tableau

To build the tableau, deal a row of seven cards, moving from left to right. The first card is dealt faceup, the rest face-down. Next, place a card on the six downcards, with the first card turned faceup. Repeat this dealing pattern until you have made seven columns (or piles) of cards ranging in count from a single card on the farthest left to seven cards on the farthest right. The top card in each column will be faceup. You can leave a slight portion of the top of each card exposed (this will indicate how many cards are still in the column), or you can square up each column into piles (this increases the difficulty of the game). All upcards in the tableau will always remain as columns. The rest of the cards form your stock, which you can keep in your hand or place on the table by the tableau.

Building

Build ascending sequences on the foundation cards (aces) and descending sequences on the cards of the tableau. Tableau sequences must be built in alternating colors, for example a ♦4 can be played on a ♠5 or ♣5. You may take cards from the stock or the tableau and place them on the foundation.

Playing

Turn over one card at a time from the stock. This card can be played on the foundation or the tableau. You can go through the stock only once. After you play a card from the stock, the prior card is now exposed and can be played, and so on until you are unable to make a play.

On the tableau, only the top card of each column (or pile) can be placed on a foundation. Any card on the tableau, however, can be moved from one column to another, but all cards below that card must move with it. For example, if you move an ♦8 on top of a ♣9 and a ♠7 and ♥6 are below the ♦8, you must move all three cards to the other column. If the ♦8 is already below the ♠9, you still may want to move only those three cards in order to expose the ♠9 because it can be placed on the ♠8 in the spade foundation.

At the beginning of play, place the ♣J on top of the ♦Q, then both of those cards on top of the ♠K, the ♥A on one of the foundation blanks above, and the ♥2 on top of the ♥A. Next, place the ♠K, ♦Q, and ♣J into the empty column, and turn over the four top downcards from the tableau.

Once a tableau column is left without an upcard, the next downcard can be turned faceup. If no downcard remains (in other words, no cards are left in this column), you can place any king from another column into this empty column. If other upcards accompany the king, they too must move into the empty column. You can also place an available king from the stock into an empty column.

The game ends when either you transfer all cards to the foundations or you go through the entire stock and have no more plays.

Tip

If you have gone halfway through the stock with little play, start a new game. Too many cards that you will need for both ascending and descending sequences have been buried. It is even safe to predict that there needs to be significant action on the board before playing from the stock to have a good chance of winning.

Variation

Some prefer to use every third card in the stock, in which case you can go through the stock as many times as you are able. The chance to win is greater in this version because it allows you to scan available cards and plan moves ahead. Luck plays a lesser role as well. As in standard play, once a card is played, the preceding card can then be played. In this variation, however, you may choose not to play an available card after considering how cards might appear when you go through the stock the next time.

CANFIELD

In the United Kingdom, solitaire card games
are called "Patience," and you certainly need
a lot of patience to succeed at Canfield,
one of the most mind-boggling of them all.

The object

On foundation cards, build an ascending sequence for each
of the four suits. You may build your sequences "round-the-
corner"; that is, the ace can follow the king and the two can
follow the ace.

The cards

Standard 52-card deck

Dealing to the tableau

Shuffle the cards. Deal out 13 cards, facedown, in a neat
stack to make your stock. Put the stock to the left side of the
table, and turn the top card faceup. The stock must always
be squared up. From the rest of the deck, take the top card
and place it faceup above and to the right of the stock. It is
the first foundation card, and it sets the starting card for all
other suits. Below the row where all your foundation cards
will sit, lay out four cards faceup to create the tableau. You
will make plays from the rest of the cards in the deck.

Building

You may add to the foundation row from the deck, the stock,
the tableau, or the discard pile. After you turn up the first
foundation card of a particular suit, the first card of the
other three suits must be of the same rank. For example, if
a ♥9 is the first foundation, you must place the 9s of spades,

diamonds, and clubs on the foundation row when they appear. Your sequence then would be 9, 10, J, Q, K, A, 2, 3, 4, 5, 6, 7, and 8 for each suit.

The tableau cards are used to build descending sequences that alternate by color. For example, a ♦6 has to be played on a ♠7 or ♣7. The descending sequences also use the round-the-corner rule. You may not have an empty space in the tableau, and an empty spot must be filled from the stock until the stock runs out. Then you can use cards from the deck. You may play the top stock card on a foundation pile

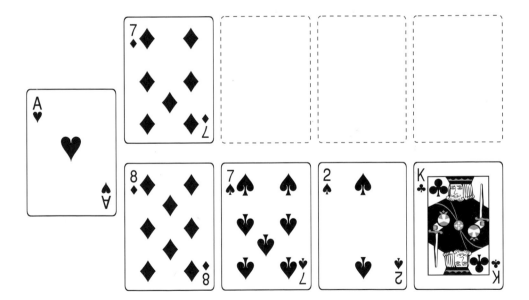

The ♦7 is the first foundation card. Place the ♠7 next to the ♦7 and the ♦8 on the top of the ♦7. Next, place the ♥A on the ♠2 and the ♣K on the ♥A. Turn the top card of the stock faceup, and fill the three empty spots in the tableau with cards from the stock before you begin play with the deck.

or on the tableau. You may also pick up an entire tableau sequence and add to another sequence in order to make an empty space. The entire unit must move together.

Playing

From the deck, turn up cards in groups of three. The top card of each group is always available to play. If you play it, the card underneath is available. Unused cards are put in a discard pile faceup. The top card of the discards is always available for play. After you run through the deck, turn the discard pile facedown, pick it up, and run through the deck again. The game continues until you've built all the foundations or you can't make any plays with the cards available to you.

Tip

It is usually better to play a card from the stock than one from the deck. Getting access to the stock cards will make it easier to build the foundations.

Variation

An easier version of this game is called Storehouse. You select the 2s from the deck and build the foundation rows before you shuffle and deal the layout. In this variation, an ace can be a curse!

ACCORDION

In this fast-paced game, you lay out the cards in a single row and fan them in and out as you make your plays.

The object

To form one faceup pile

The cards

Standard 52-card deck

Dealing to the tableau

Shuffle the cards, and deal them one at a time faceup into a single row from left to right. Because the row usually becomes quite long, you may want to create more than one row, but still treat the split row as one row.

Playing

As you deal the cards, match them by rank or suit at any time. It isn't necessary to make a match for each card you deal, but when you do, pile one card on top of another matched card, moving leftward, according to one of the following patterns: (1) If the card is next to another card of the same suit or rank, move the rightmost card on top of the leftmost card; (2) if two cards are in between the two matched cards, move the rightmost card on top of the leftmost card, leaping over the two cards in between.

Once you've made a pile, treat it as a single card. Before you play a new card from the end of the row, check to see if you've created a new move from your first.

When a newly turned card gives you two choices of moves, make whichever move seems right. Don't expect to create a single pile often; this game is even more difficult to win than Klondike.

Variations

One variation is slightly different from and more difficult than Accordion. Deal out a 13-card row. When you've completed your moves, add new cards to the right of the remaining cards until 13 cards are showing, then begin to make your matches again, and so on. You cannot show any more than 13 cards at one time. A word of warning: Do not look at the bottom of the deck before you get to the last card. That's cheating!

Another intriguing variation is Royal Marriage. You begin the game with the ♥Q on the top of the pack and the ♥K on the bottom. The deck is dealt one card at a time starting with the ♥Q. As you play, discard singletons and pairs of cards that stand between cards that match by suit or rank. If you end up with only the ♥Q and the ♥K, you've won by creating the Royal Marriage.

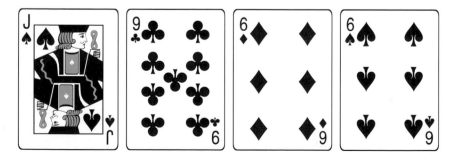

You can place the ♠6 either on top of the ♦6 or the ♠J.

VANISHING CROSS

This card game is both complex and entertaining for the avid solitaire player. It is also called Cross Currents.

The object

To build a 13-card sequence for each suit in each corner of the layout

The cards

Standard 52-card deck

Dealing to the tableau

Visualize a three-by-three square grid, like that used in a game of Tic-Tac-Toe. That is how you will lay out the cards. The four corners of the grid are where you will build the four foundation suits in ascending order. When you begin, only the upper left corner will have a card in it. You may build foundations going round-the-corner (king to ace to deuce) as needed. The five center squares of your grid— those that form a cross—are your tableau. Build sequences in these piles in descending order. There is no need to follow suit or alternate colors for tableau sequences.

Playing

Shuffle the deck, and deal a single card faceup onto each of the five squares of the tableau spaces. Next, place one card faceup onto the upper left corner. This card sets the base number for the other three foundations. The rest of the cards are your stock, from which you will turn cards faceup one at a time into a discard pile until the stock is exhausted.

You can do five things with each card you put into play from the stock:

1. Start a foundation corner.
2. Build on a foundation if it's the next higher card in the suit.
3. Build on any tableau pile.
4. Put it on any empty tableau space.
5. Add it to the discard pile.

If your first foundation card is a 7, all the other foundation cards must be 7s. Your ascending sequence will be 7-8-9-T-J-Q-K-A-2-3-4-5-6. Cards in the tableau may be played at any time, but only the top card can be moved to a foundation pile or another tableau pile. You may not take a card from a tableau and place it on the discard pile.

Only the top card of the discard pile may be put into play, and it can be placed on foundations or tableau piles. Spaces in the tableau must be kept filled as long as you have cards available. You can move one or more cards from a tableau pile, the available card from the stock, or the top discard.

Use cards from the stock one at a time. You can go through the stock only once.

In the diagram on the next page, if the next card you turn up is the ♥7, play this card in a corner location; if it's the ♥10, play it on the ♦J; or if it's the ♠2, play it on an empty tableau space or on the discard pile.

Tip

Use the empty spaces in the tableau wisely and cautiously since you have only one chance to go through the stock.

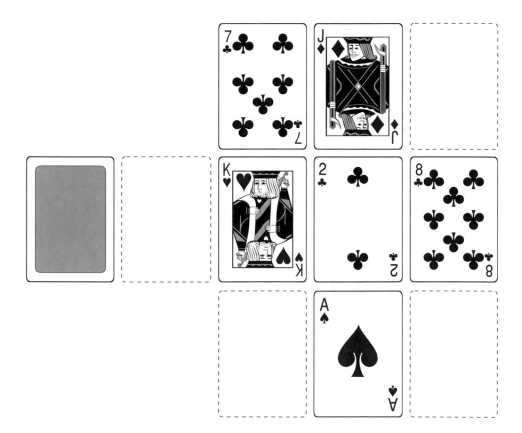

Since the ♣7 is the base card, build that entire suit in ascending sequence, ending with ♣6. Before playing a card from the stock, place the ♣8 on top of the ♣7. You can also place the ♠A on the ♣2 and then the ♥K on the ♠A, according to the descending sequence in the tableau.

PERPETUAL MOTION

Here's a game that depends on a lot of luck
but is fun because it's simple and fast moving.
It's also easy to stop and resume play later.

The object

To discard 13 four-of-a-kind sets (Suits have no bearing on this game.)

The cards

Standard 52-card deck

Dealing to the tableau

Shuffle the cards. Deal out four cards in a row faceup from left to right. The remaining 48 cards are the stock and are kept facedown.

Playing

Stack a card on top of a card of the same rank to the farthest left in the tableau. If three or four cards match, move two or three matching cards to the farthest left card. The order does not matter. Do not move a nonmatching card into an empty space but deal the next four cards from the stock in the four spaces in the tableau, which will either be empty or occupied by cards. You must always deal out from left to right.

Continue to move cards of matching rank from right to left in the tableau but only after all four cards are dealt. Only the top card can be moved—never a group of two or more cards, and never the card below the top card in the pile even if that card matches another exposed card.

Place the ♥K on top of the ♣K. Don't move the
♠6 into the vacant space. Instead, deal four
cards faceup one at a time on top of the ♥K,
♦9, empty space, and ♠6.

Once you run through the deck, gather up all the piles
to recreate the stock. First, stack the piles from right to
left; that is, place a right pile on top of a left pile until one
pile remains. Next, turn the stock facedown, and then run
through the stock again.

Each time four cards of the same rank appear at the top
of a pile, discard them into a waste pile. Continue to run
through the deck until all four-of-a-kind sets are discarded,
in which case you win, or until you reach an impasse, which
is when you run through the entire deck without the order
changing. The game is then lost.

Tips

At the stock's end, four cards should always be played on the
tableau. If not, then a misplay occurred. It's impossible to
win if the first three cards in the stock match and the fourth
matching card is the last card in the stock.

FLOWER GARDEN

Fill your garden with flowers, and see them bloom in a game that's challenging for any skilled solitaire player.

The object

To build four ascending sequences, ace (low) to king, by suit, on four foundation piles

The cards

Standard 52-card deck

Dealing to the tableau

Deal six rows of six cards below the foundation, creating six columns with each lower card placed on top of 3/4 of the preceding card. The first five rows are facedown; the last row (or top cards) is faceup. This is your "Garden" tableau. The remaining 16 cards are your "Bouquet" stock.

Playing

Turn cards from the stock faceup one at a time. When an ace appears in play—either from the tableau or the stock—place it above the tableau to begin a foundation pile in ascending sequence by suit. The tableau sequences are built in descending order in any combination of suits. Only the top card from one Garden pile may be moved to another Garden pile. When a Garden pile is emptied in the tableau, any available card can fill that space.

Play one card at a time from the Bouquet pile. You can go through this pile as many times as necessary. The game is over when you have built all four foundation sequences or when you can't make any further plays from the tableau or the stock.

Tip

Do not hurry in making a move. If you overlook a play, you can block yourself indefinitely.

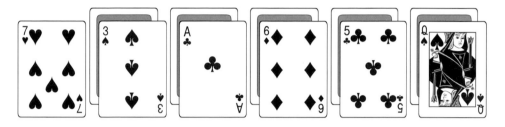

Place the ♣A above the Garden tableau to begin a foundation pile. Do not place the ♣5 on the ♦6 before putting the ♦6 on the ♥7, or you will not be able to move the ♦6 since only one card can be moved at a time.

LA BELLE LUCY

Lucy must have been quite a woman to have had this classic solitaire game named after her. Also known as "Fair Lucy" and "Midnight Oil," this card game plays out quickly and rewards players who can work out moves in advance.

The object

To build four ascending sequences, ace (low) to king, by suit

The cards

Standard 52-card deck

Dealing to the tableau

Shuffle the deck, and deal 17 packets (or fans) of three cards each, and an 18th packet of a single card. Deal the cards faceup and three at a time. These 18 packets form the tableau. Fan the packets out so the cards overlap. It is easier to play the game if you lay out your cards in five columns, with the first and final columns three rows deep, and the middle columns four rows deep.

Playing

Move only the top cards. You cannot move more than one card at a time. You can move them either to the foundation or to another tableau pile. When aces become available, move them to the foundation above the tableau to begin each foundation suit.

Tableaus are built in descending sequence by suit. When a space is created by the emptying of a packet, it is left blank. When no more play is possible, collect the cards in the tableau, shuffle these cards, and deal out to the tableau again. You may redeal the cards twice. The last packet may have less than three cards, but you must deal three cards to the preceding packets first.

Tip

Be careful not to block a card by placing a card on a packet that has a lower-ranked card of the same suit buried below.

Variation

If you play the "Three Shuffles and a Draw" version, you have one more chance to win: After the last deal, you can take one buried card and move it to another packet.

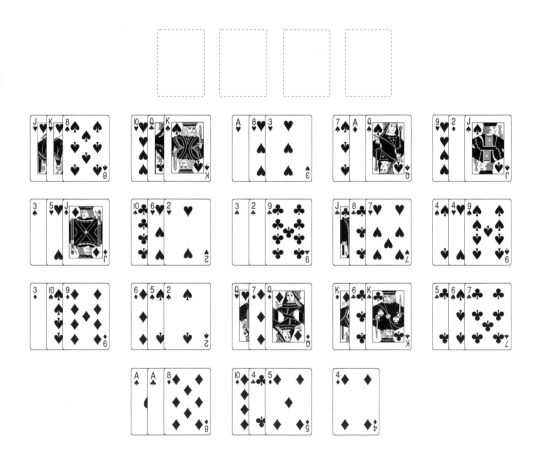

Tableau after the first deal

TUT'S TOMB

This variation of a 19th-century solitaire game called "Pyramid" likely adopted its modern name in the 1920s when King Tutankhamen's tomb was discovered. In this game, the king of spades portrays King Tut while sitting at the top of a pyramid of cards.

The object

To remove all cards from the tableau and stock by taking out kings and pairing cards whose values total 13

The cards

Standard 52-card deck

Dealing to the tableau

The top of the pyramid is the ♠K. Select it from the deck, and place it faceup on the table. After shuffling the deck, deal out cards in overlapping rows to form a pyramid. After the ♠K, the second row has two cards, and each succeeding row has an additional card until the last row has seven cards. Use the rest of the deck as your stock.

Playing

Remove all kings or pairs of cards that total 13 from the tableau. Aces count 1 each, jacks 11, queens 12, and kings 13; all other cards are valued at their rank. Since you may not play cards that are overlapped by other cards, your first plays will use only the seven cards in the last row. Remember: Both overlapping cards must be removed before a card in the row above becomes available for play.

After you flip the top card faceup from the stock, place it on top of the discard pile. You can use this card to make additional matches with available cards from the tableau. If you do, then the next upcard from the discard pile is available for play. In other words, the top card from the discard pile is always available.

Pairs and kings are laid aside separately from the discards. You can go through the stock only once.

Variation

The rules for "Pyramid" are the same except that you don't place the ♠K at the top of the pyramid.

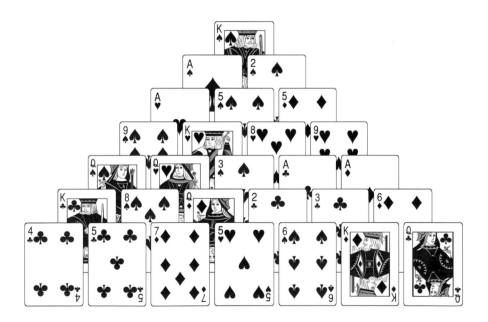

Start by removing the ♦K and using it to create a pile separate from the discard pile. Next, take the ♦7 and ♠6, which total 13, and place them on the ♦K.

SEVENTEENS

This is a strategic game for the calculating mind. Once again, skill can often beat luck.

The object

To select pairs equaling 17 or the sequence A-2-3, and then discarding them from the tableau until it is emptied and the stock is used up

The cards

Standard 52-card deck

Dealing to the tableau

Shuffle the cards, and then deal ten faceup piles of three cards each in as many rows as are convenient for you. The rest of the cards make up the stock and are placed facedown before you. In the center of the table, place three upcards from the stock next to each other in a row.

Playing

Aces count 1, jacks 11, queens 12, and kings 13; all other cards are valued at their rank. You may use only the top card of any of the ten piles or any of the three center cards. Look for pairs equaling 17 or cards in the sequence A-2-3. Place them into a discard pile. Once a center card is used, only the top card from the stock can be placed into the empty space. No card below the top card in the stock can be played. You can't place any cards in the blank spaces created by an emptied fan. You win this solitaire game when you discard all 52 cards.

Tip

Work to get cards out of the stock. That means using up the
cards in the center and replacing them frequently. The more
cards you can see, the better chance you have of planning
your future moves.

*One of your plays is discarding the ♠A, ♣2,
and ♥3. You should also remove ♥6 and ♣J,
not the ♠J, so you can fill another empty center
space with a card from the stock.*

LUCKY FOURS

An unusual solitaire game in which the odds favor the player—and not the cards. If you like to win and win often, this is the game for you.

The object

To retrieve the four aces from the tableau and build 13-card, suited sequences from ace to king

The cards

Standard 52-card deck

Dealing to the tableau

After you thoroughly shuffle the deck, deal 13 four-card fans faceup on the table, so all cards are visible. Deal three rows of three fans and two rows of two fans. (See how the cards are dealt on page 27.) The suit foundations are placed above the tableau.

Playing

Build sequences in descending order and alternate colors in the tableau. For example, a ♠6 can be placed on a ♥7, but it can't be placed on a ♣7. Move the top card or a sequence from one fan to another fan. When a fan is emptied of cards, fill the space with a single king or a sequence headed by a king. You can't fill an empty space with any other ranked card or cards. Continue to free cards by moving them to other fans or by moving them onto the foundations until you've built all four sequences in the foundation or you are blocked.

A typical way of dealing out the tableau.
Begin by placing the ♥A and ♣A above
the tableau to begin the suit foundations.

THE SULTAN OF TURKEY

This fascinating, two-deck game usually results in success for the player. Your goal is to build a "seraglio" for the Sultan, who is portrayed by the king of hearts. A "seraglio" is a harem—in this case, the Sultan wants a harem of eight queens.

The object

To build suit sequences that ascend from the ace to the queen on the seven outside kings and from the deuce to the queen on the ♥A (Cards are not built on the center ♥K, which represents the Sultan of Turkey and must always be by itself and remain visible.)

The cards

Two 52-card decks (It does not matter if the backs of the decks are not alike.)

Dealing to the tableau

Remove the eight kings and the ♥A from the decks. All these cards are arranged in three rows of three. Place a ♥K in the center of the middle row, with the ♥A in the row beneath the ♥K. The cards surrounding the ♥K are the foundations. Next, deal a column of four upcards on each side of the kings. The tableau cards are available to play on the foundations. The remaining cards form the stock.

Playing

Play tableau cards on the suit foundations. Then turn up the top card from the stock, and place it on top of the

discard pile. If possible, place this card on the suit foundations or an empty tableau space. The top card from the discard pile is always available. After you go through the stock, you may go through the discard pile twice, but don't shuffle the discards—just turn them facedown and go through them one at a time.

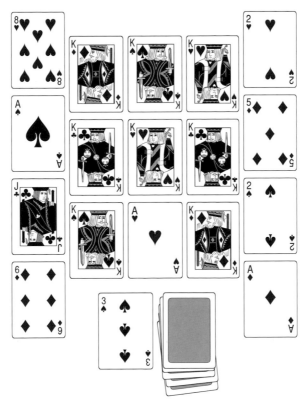

Place the ♦A on either ♦Ks, the ♠A on either ♠Ks, and the ♥2 on the ♥A. Next, place the ♠2 on the ♠A, and take the ♠3 from the discard pile and put it on the ♠2. You can use the next card from the top of the discard pile to add to a foundation pile or to fill an empty tableau space. Or you can turn up the next card from the stock and use that card for either purpose.

SPIDER

This game is one of the most mentally challenging solitaires.

The object

To remove every card from the tableau by building eight descending suited piles in the tableau from king to ace

The cards

Two 52-card decks. (It does not matter if the backs of the decks are not alike.)

Dealing to the tableau

Deal a row of ten downcards and then three rows of ten downcards on top of the first row, with buried cards slightly exposed. In this way, you can determine how many cards are still remaining in each column. Next, deal an additional downcard to the first four columns. Finally, deal one upcard on top of each column, while still slightly exposing the buried cards. The stock comprises the remaining 50 cards of the two decks.

Playing

All the action is in the tableau. Regardless of suit, an upcard can be played on an upcard one rank above it. As a unit, a sequence in the same suit can be moved to another stack. Otherwise, cards are moved singly. No card can be placed on an ace, and any card or suited sequence can be placed in an emptied space in the tableau.

Whenever a downcard is uncovered, turn it up and play it if you can. When you run out of moves or choose not to